YELLOWSTONE

125 Years

OF AMERICA'S BEST IDEA

by Michael Milstein

Billings Gazette
The Source.

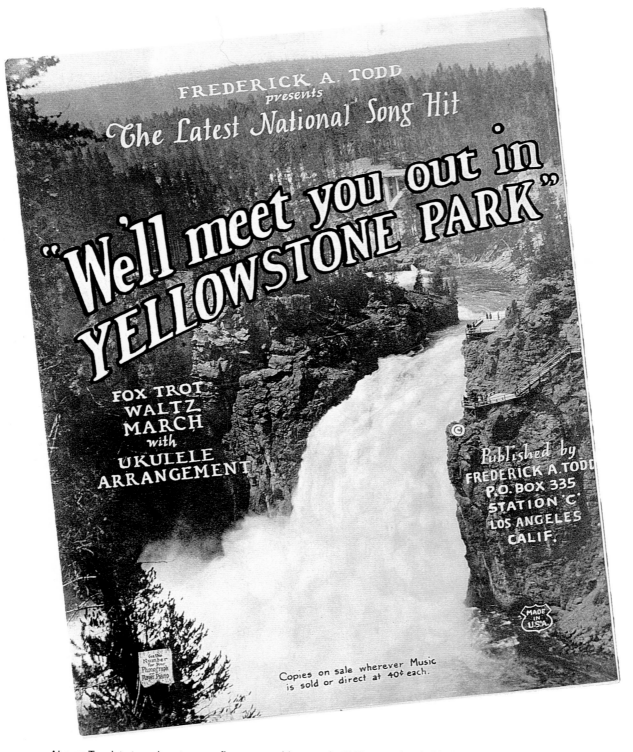

Above: Tourists tuned up to campfire songs with an early 1900s song book titled "We'll Meet You Out in Yellowstone Park."

Title page: A photo by William H. Jackson depicts the highway through the Golden Gate south of Mammoth Hot Springs in 1902.

Front cover: A calendar from 1912 depicts an Army cavalryman with two tourists at Mammoth Hot Springs.

Back cover: A William Jackson photo from 1902 shows the Lower Falls of the Yellowstone.

Published by The Billings Gazette
Wayne Schile, Publisher
Richard J. Wesnick, Editor

© 1996, The Billings Gazette

Written by Michael Milstein, reporter, The Billings Gazette
Edited by Richard J. Wesnick

ISBN 0-9627618-9-3   Library of Congress catalog card number 96-078550

For additional copies of this book contact:
The Billings Gazette, P.O. Box 36300, Billings, MT, 59107-6300.
In Billings, call 657-1200. Or call toll-free from outside Billings, 1-800-543-2707

The Giant.

Giant Geyser spews water and steam in this 1902 photo by William H. Jackson.

The arch at Yellowstone Park's northern entrance near Mammoth has welcomed visitors since 1903.

Contents

Foreword 8

Fire and Brimstone 13

Marking the Spot 33

Come One, Come All 57

Changing Times 83

Acknowledgements 110

Credits 111

For Further Reading 112

The Hayden Survey of 1871 documented the wonders of Yellowstone Park in volumes that now reside in the Park archives at Mammoth.

Above: A bluebird's colorful plumage stands out against the greenery of the park.

Left: Yellowstone Lake is one of the largest high-altitude lakes in the world.

T he national park idea, the best idea we ever had, was inevitable as soon as Americans learned to confront the wild continent not with fear and cupidity but with delight, wonder and awe.

Wallace Stegner, Western novelist-essayist, 1983

Foreword

Yellowstone is a place and it is also an idea. One hundred twenty-five years ago, a decision was made by the people of the United States, acting through their Congress. On the basis of that idea, we sent in the cavalry to rescue from exploitation a landscape of wonder—and a very big place.

The idea was that some portions of our vast national patrimony would belong to all of us, and would be saved for all of us, from all other uses except being themselves. The parks are ends—not means. They are of absolute value. They are not merely of conditional value.

Parks are important to us not for what can be done to them or with them, not for what they might yield in metals or oil or lumber, nor for what they could be turned into—parking lots or condos or strip malls or even office parks. They are valued for what they are. The 125th anniversary of Yellowstone reminds us of that idea. Seven years earlier, in 1865, our greatest president, Abraham Lincoln, asserted that Yosemite would be saved. At Yellowstone, in 1872, Lincoln's idea became a fixed national policy.

The Yellowstone idea is a generous one, and a patriotic one. It requires us to save for common purposes, for everybody, some of this land. And not just a little bit of wonder here and another bit there. We save enough to be an entire, healthy, living environment, having enough size to have integrity. And the Yellowstone idea is that no single person will be able to keep all others out. It will remain whole, protected and preserved, to remind us of the glories of this "great estate"—Lincoln's term for our American land. And that idea carried an obligation—Yellowstone's integrity will be preserved by us all.

Yellowstone is big. Big enough to let those of us who love to hike there breathe freely, stretch our legs and arms and feel space. The other animals with which we co-inhabit that space need amplitude—and so do we. In our cities, we feel, too often, confined and cramped, anxious—and unwanted. But in Yellowstone we tread our own ample earth, free in a place that belongs to all of us. We have a right to be there and we feel welcome there.

We in the National Park Service are honored to be the trustees for the rest of the American people in preserving Yellowstone, and the Yellowstone idea, for our descendants. We thank those who brought it to us 125 years ago. We renew our commitment to the place, and to the idea.

Roger Kennedy
Director, National Park Service, 1993-1997

The Yellowstone River plunges over the Lower Falls into the Grand Canyon of the Yellowstone.

Tourists in days gone by crowded close to Old Faithful Geyser.

Photographs - Mrs. Arch Robison, Columbus, Ohio while honeymooning in Yellowstone 1916

"Don't feed the bears" says the warning, but photos from an old scrapbook show this tourist ignoring it in 1916.

Above: The Firehole River meanders past the steaming Midway Geyser Basin.

Facing page: Western artist Thomas Moran poses among the Mammoth Hot Springs terraces in this photo from the Hayden Survey in 1871.

Fire and Brimstone

There is a place in the heart of Yellowstone where we do not reign.

It is a place nestled among lodgepole pines, next to hot springs, all popping, fizzling and burping an earthen medley. One little crater spits bits of mud, building a clay-colored shelf that might qualify as the newest earth on Earth. On cold days, steam rises in curtains. Sulfurous fumes ebb and flow with the breeze and, as Mark Twain said, are not altogether unpleasant, at least to a sinner.

Heat pouring from the earth has killed a few trees. Their branches stand bare. Some have fallen and stretch across the ground, fusing with the earth as they decay into dark soil as soft and rich as pile carpet.

Bison seem to like this place. Their bulldozer heads and humped backs paint outlines, like a field of boulders, against the steam rolling over them. Their exhalations add to it. When snow falls, it frosts their fur and they dissolve amid the vapor. Bones disclose that a few beasts have died and dissolved altogether.

Fresh snow betrays the tracks of a hulking grizzly bear that has padded by a few minutes before. It's hard to resist holding a hand over one of the hard-packed, deeply clawed depressions only to find that any one of them swallows the hand whole.

It's refreshing, even to those who never see it, to know this place exists. A place where a human's presence can be swallowed up, where we are not in charge. This is the gift of Yellowstone National Park, a grand gift we gave to ourselves 125 years ago.

It may not be precisely the kind of gift President Ulysses S. Grant had in mind on March 1, 1872 when he signed the bill that invented national parks by turning Yellowstone into the world's first. There had never been a national park before. Anywhere. Sure, there had been game preserves in Europe, nicely tended neighborhood parks, but there had never been a place protected for its own sake. Nobody knew just what Yellowstone was, or what it should or would become. We have since found within it our own biological, geological and philosophical treasures that might have otherwise gone unknown. Only with time has its gift reached beyond the dark lines that denote boundaries on a map and into our minds and hearts.

Empires are built on power and control. But the proudest empire is not one over which we have amassed power and control, even though we could have. Instead, it is one over which we have relinquished control, one where we have agreed to step down from our pedestal. An empire that belongs not to us, but to our future.

It is easier to protect a place we rule than it is to protect one we do not, yet that is what we have done—what we are doing—in Yellowstone.

Clouds of controversy swirl from time to time, debates heat up and scientists break Yellowstone down into components and theories. But no matter how it's disassembled and

The Park Museum holds many artifacts, including this photo album of a wedding trip through Yellowstone in 1906.

A snowshoed traveler gazes at the frozen Lower Falls in mid-winter 1893.

Right: Yellowstone Park's first human inhabitants were Native Americans who used projectile points such as these to hunt wildlife.

Facing page: The rising sun casts a warm glow over Abiathar Peak.

reassembled on paper, there is nothing quite like Yellowstone as a whole—a whole that does not exist on maps. Power flows from the geysers and mud pots, the vast wildlife herds, the landscape beyond the park boundaries and through the national forests that surround them, spreading the national park ideal throughout the world. As a lightning rod, Yellowstone has generated enough sparks to illuminate the intricacies of wildlife management, wildfires, wilderness and the notion of a true ecosystem, teaching us much about the natural world and our place within it. The greatest anniversary present we could give to this raw portrait of nature would be our pledge to continue learning from it.

Letting Yellowstone be does not mean keeping it the same. Sameness is not in Yellowstone's dictionary. The watchword is change—relentless and forceful change; Yellowstone insists on it.

Which is its beauty.

Yellowstone is the way it is because of the world below it. Subterranean furnaces stoked by the intense pressure of the earth burn hot beneath Yellowstone, firing a landscape that reflects them. Today's geysers are evidence of that deep-seated heat, which is not always so benign. Sometimes the heat and pressure intensify until their only release is through a thunderous explosion, the last one of which hit about 600,000 years ago, leaving a giant crater that encompasses the heart of today's Yellowstone. The dark volcanic bulwarks that line the southern edge of the Madison River are vestiges of the crater rim and continue to rattle with earthquakes even today.

It is a place that commandeered our imagination from the start, that inspired us to break new ground in the then-undefined field of conservation as powerfully as a geyser blasting from a sapphire pool. Even in an age where wilderness was commonplace, where wild animals were plentiful, when the national will favored expansion and development over restraint and preservation, Yellowstone impressed everyone it touched as a special place, leading its audience to fight for nothing more and nothing less than an assurance that it would be and will be left alone.

For it was, in a word, unbelievable.

Nobody knows either the identity of the first people to see Yellowstone, or what they thought of it. A different climate molded the region then and those early visitors were more familiar with mammoths than with today's elk or bison. In more recent times, American

Indians trailed wild game through the region and a small population of Native Americans known as the Sheepeaters (for their appetite for bighorn sheep) eventually lived in what we know today as the first national park. Chunks from Obsidian Cliff were in great demand as raw material for their hand-made arrowheads.

Early tales imply that Indian tribes avoided Yellowstone because they were somehow afraid of Yellowstone's bizarre geological phenomena, thinking them the wrath of angry deities. But archaeologists have found enough leftover projectile points and other artifacts at settlement sites along the shores of Yellowstone Lake and in other spots to conclude that early peoples did not keep their distance from Yellowstone. Instead, they frequented Yellowstone for many years, probably relishing many of the same qualities we do today.

In its probing of the West, the Lewis and Clark Expedition picked up hints of a great volcano that emits "a loud noise like thunder, which makes the earth tremble" to the south of the route the party blazed through Montana. But they did not seek out the reality behind the rumblings. Perhaps they disregarded the hubbub in the same way one might toss away an uncut geode, never realizing the wonder lying within it.

Bits and pieces filtered out. In 1805, the governor of the land the United States had bought from France under the Louisiana Purchase two years earlier wrote to President Thomas Jefferson. In a curiously halting and qualified way, he told the president that a map of the new real estate "is not destitute of Interests, as it exposes the location of several important Objects, & may point the way to useful enquiry—among other things a little incredible, a volcano is distinctly described on Yellow Stone River."

It was incredible. And in a roundabout way, the images of spouting springs and steaming plains were so incredible that they served to safeguard Yellowstone while a younger America parceled out its western frontier.

Those Indians and trappers who knew the place were few in number and even scarcer in influence. One of the earliest was John Colter, a tough graduate of the Lewis and Clark

1300. A Native Growler, Yellowstone Park.

An old stereo viewing card offers a three-dimensional view of a Park bear.

A bull elk wades across the pristine Madison River.

A photo from the 1871 Hayden Survey shows the mirror-smooth surface of Yellowstone Lake.

Expedition who an acquaintance said carried "an open, ingenious, and pleasant countenance of the Daniel Boone stamp." A cryptic reference to "Hot Spring Brimstone" on a crude map Colter devised following an 1808 trek through the territory brought him notoriety as the first white man to detect at least a trace of the fantastic contents of Yellowstone. But it was not until 1827 that the first written description of the place appeared in a Philadelphia newspaper. It was likely considered fiction.

Following skirmishes with Blackfeet Indians, a beaver trapper named Daniel T. Potts wrote to his brother of a freshwater lake "on the verry top of the mountain which is about one hundred by forty Miles in diameter and as clear as crystal." If there is any doubt Potts was describing Yellowstone Lake, it vanishes with the next sentence.

> *On the south borders of this lake is a number of hot and boiling springs some of water and others of most beautiful fine clay and resembles that of a mush pot and throws its particles to the immense height of from twenty to thirty feet in height. The clay is white and of a pink, and water appears fathomless as it appears to be entirely hollow under neath. There is also a number of places where the pure suphor [sulfur] is sent forth in abundance one of our men Visited one of those wilst taking his recreation there at an instan the earth began a tremendious trembling and he with difficulty made his escape when an explosion took place resembling that of thunder.*

On a short excursion to the north "for the purpose of accumalating a few more Bever" Potts and his fellows encountered another band of Blackfeet but found "our enemy as much allarmed as ourselves."

Ages ago, without the modern handholds of today, without the explanatory signs now

A rainbow seems to rise from the waters of Yellowstone Lake.

A foolhardy, olden-day tourist peers over the edge of Giantess Geyser, which erupts up to 200 feet in height.

planted amid the geyser basins, those who saw Yellowstone must have found themselves drunk with wonder. It shows in their writings. A young trapper talked of cresting a hill "and behold! The whole country beyond was smoking with the vapor from boiling springs, and burning with gasses, issuing from small craters, each of which was emitting a sharp whistling sound." Grasping for a human handle on the wild scene, he likened it to a winter view of the city of Pittsburgh.

Warren Angus Ferris, an American Fur Company clerk, was so taken by the tales he had heard of Yellowstone, he sought the truth. He arrived among the geysers after dark. When he arose,

> *clouds of vapor seemed like a dense fog to over-hang the springs, from which frequent reports or explosions of different loudness, constantly assailed our ears. I immediately proceeded to inspect them, and might have exclaimed with the Queen of Sheba, when their full reality of dimensions and novelty burst upon my view, "The half was not told me."*

A decal commemorated the Park's 75th anniversary.

Ferris was the first to identify certain of Yellowstone's thermal features as "geysers," a term that had originated in geyser-spouting Iceland. He stuck his hand in the basin of one of the fantastic fountains and yanked it out, explaining diplomatically that the heat, smell, and "unearthly rumbling under the rock on which I stood so ill accorded with my notions of personal safety, that I retreated back precipitately to a respectful distance." It probably burned, too. Indians who accompanied Ferris were reasonably appalled by his advances on the springs: "One of them remarked that hell, of which he had heard from the whites, must be in the vicinity." He blamed their wariness on a fear of evil spirits, but anyone who knows Yellowstone and its scalding springs might more accurately attribute it to plain old common sense.

As captivating as they were, such descriptions seem to have fallen through the cracks of the national conscience. Partly, perhaps, because their unbelievable air mixed with official reports dismissing the American West as a wasteland with no use but as a pasture for the tremendous herds of buffalo that roamed there. However false the notion, the misinformation conferred a protective shroud of obscurity over the great wildernesses of the Northern Rockies until a youthful United States had matured and could begin to weigh the inestimable value of a spectacular land left to itself.

Even when whispers of Yellowstone filtered out of the forests of the West, few people believed them. Facing such skepticism, those in the know embellished what would seem to be unembellishable, perhaps figuring they might as well give the skeptics something to be skeptical about.

Among tellers of tall tales, the famous frontiersman Jim Bridger stood head and shoulders above the rest. In a photograph, his wrinkled neck and ragged beard lend him a stony

Photographer William Jackson caught the many hues of a Park hot pool in 1902.

look far more serious than his yarns. He told of stumbling into a mountain of glass that we know as Obsidian Cliff, a place where a man could holler across an expanse so wide and resonant the echo would return to wake him in the morning and a hot spring—maybe not so far-fetched—where a fish caught in cold water would be cooked to order on its way through searing currents near the surface. While Bridger probably didn't originate every tall tale attributed to him, each fits his character. His tallest tale of all may have sprung out of fossil-laden Specimen Ridge, where Bridger promised "I'll show you peetrified trees a-growing, with peetrified birds on 'em a-singing peetrified songs."

Outlandish tales like Bridger's probably added to Yellowstone's geographical camouflage.

What finally inspired official explorations of the little known corner of the map was not so much a quest for knowledge as it was a quest for material treasure.

In the late summer of 1863, 42 men joined engineer Walter DeLacy on his incursion into the largely unknown landscape.

They saw strange and fantastic sights. Steaming holes in the ground. Rivers slithering through rainbow colored canyons. Wildlife galore. But they caught no glimpses of what they were really looking for: gold.

It must have been disappointing. DeLacy did not bother to publish his journal of the trip until years later. He must have figured nobody would be very interested.

We might wonder how anyone could prospect in the region that today cradles Yellowstone National Park and discover no more than disappointment. It's a discrepancy that changes with the perspective of time. Wild places mean something different to us than they did to DeLacy and his followers. We who visit the first national park today would probably agree that its assembled contents are worth infinitely more than gold—worth more, in many different senses, than an explorer like DeLacy could have ever imagined.

Souvenirs have kept memories of trips to Yellowstone alive for millions of tourists.

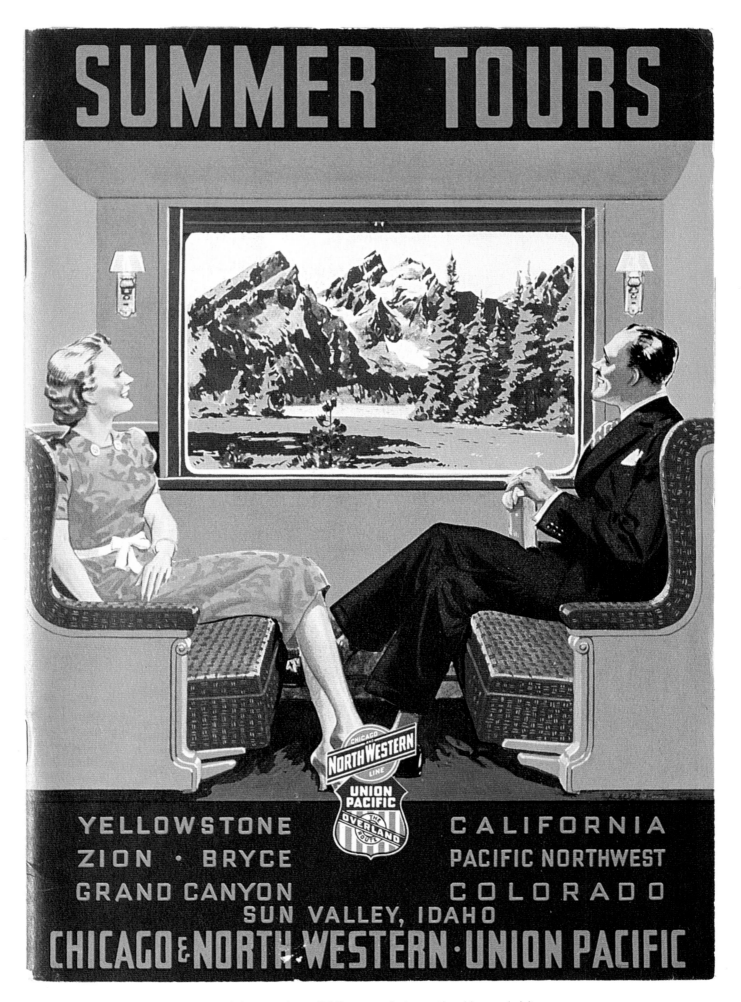

Railroad posters across the nation touted the attractions of Yellowstone Park to entice riders and visitors.

1310. Grand Falls of Yellowstone River, 360 Feet High, from Bottom of Canon, Yellowstone Park.

A stereo card shows the Lower Falls of the Yellowstone River in three dimensions.

1295. The New Glass Road at Base of Obsidian Cliffs, Yellowstone Park.

A stagecoach travels along the New Glass Road at the base of Obsidian Cliff.

Orange flames of color stream from the deep blue heart of Grand Prismatic Spring.

Above: Bison breath hangs in the air on a cold morning in Yellowstone.

Left: Tower Creek flows from rocky minarets and drops 132 feet into the Yellowstone River.

Right: An early poster from the Chicago and North Western Railway shows Old Faithful Geyser.

Below: Artist Thomas Moran used charcoal to create a dramatic sketch of Index Peak near the northeast entrance to Yellowstone Park in 1905.

Tourists at Brink of Upper Falls

Tourists watched the Yellowstone River crash over the Upper Falls in this photo from before the turn of the century.

The Yellowstone River rages through the Grand Canyon of the Yellowstone, one of the most spectacular gorges in the world.

Marking the Spot

*I*t was a difficult choice for Captain William F. Raynolds of the U.S. Army's short-lived Corps of Geographical Engineers. He was on a tight schedule to observe a solar eclipse in July of 1860 and to identify passages between the Wind River and Missouri River drainages and had hoped the mission would take him through the intriguing Yellowstone region. To his credit, Raynolds had even detected a thread of truth in Jim Bridger's tales of spouting springs that resembled the geysers of Iceland: "As he is uneducated and has probably never heard of the existence of such natural marvels elsewhere, I have little doubt that he spoke of that which he had actually seen."

Although Raynolds had Bridger as a guide, the party ran into a divide so imposing that Bridger, in an I-told-you-so tone, said "A bird can't fly over that without taking a supply of grub along."

On the cusp of an alluring blank spot on the map, Raynolds turned back in frustration, glumly conceding that he regarded "the valley of the Upper Yellowstone as the most interesting unexplored district of our widely expanded country."

Others would prove it so.

Colorful stories of Yellowstone inspired a few influential imaginations. Artist George Catlin is believed to have entered Yellowstone and afterwards he

Photographer William Jackson produced this dramatic photo of Giant Geyser in 1902. "Giant" erupts as high as 300 feet, expelling more than a million gallons of water.

talked of "a large reservation of public land to be a Nation's Park, containing man and beast in all the wildness and freshness of their natural beauty." A priest who had described the place to Francis Meagher, then governor of the Montana Territory, wrote later that the governor had replied, "if things were as described the government ought to reserve the territory for a national park."

A postcard with a Yellowstone Park postmark over a 1-cent stamp carried news from a tourist in 1908.

They knew not the value of their thoughts.

Skirmishes with Indians known to scalp their victims and the Civil War drained the resolve of official expeditions to Yellowstone until three worn-out mine workers named David E. Folsom, Charles W. Cook and William Peterson set out in 1869. They departed with five horses, knives, guns, fishing tackle, 175 pounds of flour, 30 pounds of sugar and other provisions. A friend advised: "Good-bye boys, look out for your hair."

What surfaces within their simple words is a deep respect for what they saw, a sense that even in an age that promoted the conquest of the West, they recognized that some designs fell beyond humanity's reach. And the precedent that they set with such respect, perhaps more than anything else, laid the groundwork for the idea that a national park, unknown at the time, could truly come to be.

Arriving at the Grand Canyon of the Yellowstone, the trio found themselves blanketed under a September snow that did not dampen their curiosity. They heard the howls of wolves, the roars of mountain lions, the bugling of elk. On the brink of the canyon, Cook later wrote, "I sat there in amazement, while my companions came up, and after that, it seemed to me it was five minutes before anyone spoke." When Folsom saw the roaring falls at the upper end of the canyon, he knew not to try and replicate it in words. "Language is inadequate to convey a just conception of the awful grandeur and sublimity of this masterpiece of nature's handiwork." Mud Volcano broadcast its presence with belches that carried a half-mile. The Yellowstone Lake inlet now known as Bridge Bay "was one of the beautiful places we had found fashioned by the practised hand of nature, that man had not desecrated." They seemed eerily aware of what the future held,

> for this inland sea, its crystal waves dancing and sparkling in the sunlight as if laughing with joy for their wild freedom. It is a scene of transcendent beauty which has been viewed by few white men, and we felt glad to have looked upon it before its primeval solitude should be broken by the crowds of pleasure seekers which at no distant day will throng its shores.

An ash tray from the Navy's U.S.S. *Yellowstone* is one of the more unusual mementos in the Park's archives.

Cook and Folsom wrote an article about what they had seen and promptly began collect-

A hardy sketch artist was photographed at Norris Geyser Basin in mid-winter.

The Hayden Survey team camped on the shore of Yellowstone Lake in 1871.

ing rejection slips. Neither the New York Tribune nor the magazine Scribner's would wager their reputations by publishing what they called, "such unreliable material."

On Yellowstone's golden anniversary, Cook recalled that during their 1869 trek through the region, he, Folsom and Peterson had mourned the inevitable exploitation of the region.

> *I said that I thought the place was too big to be all taken up, but that, anyway, something ought to be done to keep the settlers out, so that everyone who wanted to, in future years, could travel through as freely and enjoy the region as we had. Then Folsom said, "The government ought not to allow anyone to locate here at all."*
>
> *"That's right," I said. "It ought to be kept for the public some way."*
>
> *None of us definitely suggested the idea of a national park. National parks were unknown then. But we knew that as soon as the wonderful character of the country was generally known outside, there would be plenty of people hurrying in to get possession, unless something was done.*

Something would soon be done. Henry D. Washburn, surveyor-general of the Montana territory, collected details from Folsom and arranged an expedition of nine men. They hit the trail in August 1870 and quickly penetrated the heart of Yellowstone, which threw them one trial after another. Several of the men grew sick, they believed, from drinking toxic hot-spring water or breathing noxious fumes—although the more likely culprit was poorly canned peaches. Lt. Gustavus C. Doane, head of the group's military escort, had an injured thumb infected so badly he could hardly sleep. Nathaniel P. Langford, who had joined the party after losing a political plum of a posting in

An early Park ranger badge.

An old photo album cover shows the world's most famous geyser, Old Faithful.

Echinus Geyser is one of the most regular and frequent performers among the ranks of Yellowstone geysers.

Montana, got entangled in the rope of a horse that dragged him into a log and, later, nearly boiled himself in a hot spring. And finally, Truman C. Everts got hopelessly lost in the very untamed wilderness his group was trying to chart.

Luck quickly abandoned Everts after he and the others lost each other in thick timber south of Yellowstone Lake. His horse then ran off with his rifle, blankets, food, matches and spare clothes. Then he lost his eyeglasses. He burned his thigh in a hot spring and his toes got frostbitten. His only meal was the stringy roots of a native plant that later came to be known—in a strange sort of tribute to the hapless wanderer—as the Everts thistle. More than a month later, two mountaineers realized that an injured bear they had come across was actually the missing explorer, frail, nearly frozen and barely able to speak.

It is, perhaps, telling that even as Yellowstone reduced Everts to a crumpled shadow of a man, the place led his compatriots to one of the greatest ideas in the history of conservation.

The burst of genius is now memorialized in a fable as evocative and shadowy as those tales that had seeped out of the land of geysers for decades before. A group of rugged, worn men, clustered around a campfire near today's Madison Junction in the shadow of the point that bears the name National Park Mountain. Talk turning to the profits that would accompany control of plots of land at such strategic sites as the grand waterfalls of the Grand Canyon of the Yellowstone and the majestic spouts—Old Faithful, Beehive, Giantess—of the Upper Geyser Basin. Langford later recounted the discussion:

> *Mr. [Cornelius] Hedges then said that he did not approve of any of these plans—that there ought to be no private ownership of any portion of that region, but the whole ought to be set apart as a great National Park, and each one of us ought to make an effort to have this accomplished.*

Like most legends, this one may be a blend of both fact and fiction. It seems unlikely that Hedges, an esteemed attorney, expressed the idea in such royal form; his daily diary mentions nothing at all about a conversation so momentous that its consequences would have drowned out the crashing of nearby Firehole Falls. But somehow the party in all its clumsiness—maybe even because of that clumsiness—found itself stumbling around a corner for

the first time, recognizing that the value of a fascinating spot on the map may be best maximized not by extracting dollars from it, but by forsaking those dollars for something much more valuable. Instead of setting out to conquer the place that had dealt them so much misfortune, members of the Washburn party set out to save it—so we, too, could confront it as they did.

Langford unintentionally explained why when he wrote of returning to Mud Volcano

> *for the one especial purpose, among others of a general nature, of assuring myself that the notes made in my diary a few days ago are not exaggerated.*
>
> *No! they are not! The sensations inspired in me to-day, on again witnessing its convulsions, and the dense clouds of vapor expelled in rapid succession from its crater, amid the jarring of the earth, and the ominous intonations from belief, were those of mingled dread and wonder. At war with all former experience it was so novel, so unnaturally natural, that I feel while now writing and thinking of it, as if my own senses might have deceived me with a mere figment of the imagination. But it is not so.*

As Hedges wrote later, "I think a more confirmed set of skeptics never went out into the wilderness than those who composed our party, and never was a party more completely surprised and captivated with the wonders of nature."

Their wonder was infectious. Among the first to succumb to it was Ferdinand V. Hayden, a Civil

Motorists encountered both impressive wildlife and challenging one-way roads on their rides through Yellowstone.

War surgeon and the charismatic head of the nation's new geological survey. After hearing Langford lecture in Washington, D.C., Hayden pulled strings in Congress to win himself $40,000 for another official expedition to Yellowstone. This time, it was no rag-tag bunch. It included geologists, botanists and zoologists, as well as photographer William H. Jackson and artist Thomas Moran. Jackson's photos and Moran's brilliant watercolors would become two of the expedition's greatest contributions to Yellowstone: visual proof of the sights that had seemed so elusive for so long.

Handing out new names to the sights as it went (Hayden Valley would come later), the Hayden expedition of 1871 was taken by the same views we are today. Jackson's riveting photographs catalog the spots. Grotto Geyser. Crystal Falls on Cascade Creek. The Mammoth terraces. Old Faithful. Yellowstone Lake. The turquoise bloom, fringed with yellows and deep oranges, that is Grand Prismatic Spring. Just as striking was an earthquake that rattled the group at its encampment, reminding its 34 men of the restless earth beneath their feet.

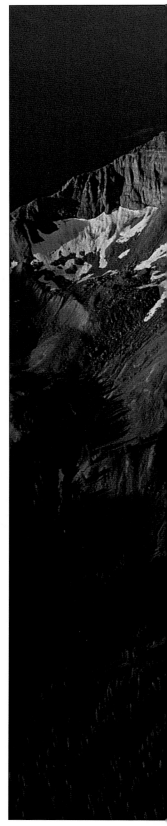

And upon their return they rattled Washington, D.C., telling Congress that a special place deserved special attention.

The government had earlier transferred the granite-walled Yosemite Valley to the State of California with the goal of preserving its natural splendor. But the bureaucratic wheels had not

An unfinished sketch of the Lower Canyon of the Yellowstone by Western artist Thomas Moran.

yet ground out a precedent for a National Park, a place of such caliber it ought to be reserved for all the people of the country—and of the world.

In a 500-page report to Congress, Hayden crystallized the suggestion that had been awaiting the right opportunity.

He said: It is time.

A bill, motivated by many forces, appeared in Congress. Montana leaders wanted a national park so Wyoming could not claim Yellowstone as its own attraction. Railroad executives favored a tourist draw that would lure more passengers aboard their trains to the West. Agriculture and mining interests, in a propitious extension of the Great Western Wasteland theory, decided Yellowstone had little value to them. An influential congressman (for whose daughter the Hayden survey had named the makeshift boat it used to plumb Yellowstone Lake) shepherded the measure along. Proponents assured Congress the establishment of a public reserve would require no financial appropriations.

But such intricacies dissolve before the raw power of the idea itself.

Snow laces the rugged heights of Amphitheater Mountain well into the summer.

A plume of steam mirrors the finely woven channels that carry water away from Firehole Lake.

Souvenir postcards show the tent facilities offered to tourists by Wylie's "Permanent Camping Co."

In the end, it matters little who was the first to put it in words, to promote it or to pursue it. Preserving a slice of the natural world might have been new to us at the time, but it was not new to the concert of primeval forces that alone had cast Yellowstone from a different and one-time mold, erecting geographical, topographical and philosophical barriers against its plundering in whatever form. It might best be said that the concept of a national park—whatever that meant at the time—originally sprang, like Old Faithful, from the land itself, a land that earned its rightful reverence from nearly every thinking person who had encountered it.

Hayden realized in a report (confidently containing a hand-drawn map with the title, "Yellowstone National Park") that the as-yet-unpassed bill would stake out a turning point in the thinking of a populace that had seized upon schemes to squeeze profit from the West. At a time when every man could have his own piece of the frontier, he predicted, the measure would reserve a piece of the frontier for Everyman. It will, wrote the effective lobbyist who resembled Abraham Lincoln,

> mark an era in the popular advancement of scientific thought, not only in this country, but throughout the civilized world.
>
> That our legislators, at a time when public opinion is so strong against appropriating the public domain for any purpose however laudable, should reserve, for the benefit and instruction of the people, a tract of 3,578 square miles, is an act that should cause universal joy throughout the land.
>
> This noble deed may be regarded as a tribute from our legislators to science, and the gratitude of the nation and of men of science in all parts of the world is due them for this munificent donation.

A Congressional committee recommended urgent protection:

This whole region was, in comparatively modern geological times, the scene of the most wonderful volcanic activity of any portion of our country. The hot springs and the geysers represent the last stages—the vents or escape pipes—of these remarkable manifestations of the internal forces. All these springs are adorned with decorations more beautiful than human art ever conceived, and which have required thousands of years for the cunning hand of nature to form. Persons are now waiting for the spring to open to enter in and take possession of these remarkable curiosities, to make merchandise of these beautiful specimens, to fence in these rare wonders, so as to charge visitors a fee, as is now done at Niagara Falls, for the sight of that which ought to be as free as the air or water.

Albums embossed in gold and containing the best of Jackson's almost 400 photographs of Yellowstone's most striking sites and sights appeared on the desks of members of Congress as they prepared to cast their vote on the first national park bill ever. They passed it and on March 1, 1872, President U.S. Grant signed his name to the handwritten measure, outlining a great square within and among the high peaks of the Northern Rockies, "to set apart a certain tract of land lying near the head waters of the Yellowstone River as a public park."

The tract was "dedicated and set apart as a public park or pleasuring-ground for the benefit and enjoyment of the people." The Secretary of the Interior was to ensure the preservation of "all timber, mineral deposits, natural curiosities, or wonders within said park, and their retention in their natural condition."

That was it. No further instructions came with the new national park. It had no one to run it, no real laws to protect it, no particular mission to guide it, not even a government-sanctioned name. It was left to find itself in a spirited search that continues to this day, a search as rocky and unpredictable as a cranky grizzly bear, a search that is as much in our minds as it is in the terrain that had so easily proved its wildness to poor Truman Everts. But there was no need to search for the single, strident power the unequaled place would cement through its lifetime, that would more than make up for whatever elements it might, in its youth, have been missing.

For Yellowstone's strongest ally was, and still is, the will and the love of the people.

One of the earliest letters to describe Yellowstone Park was written in 1827 by Daniel Potts.

A dramatic sunset sweeps across Midway Geyser Basin.

YELLOWSTONE NATIONAL PARK.
PUBLISHED BY F. JAY HAYNES.

YELLOWSTONE NATIONAL PARK.
PUBLISHED BY F. JAY HAYNES.

OLD FAITHFUL GEYSER DURING ERUPTION.
YELLOWSTONE NATIONAL PARK.

THE LAND OF GEYSERS

YELLOWSTONE PARK SEASON 1906.
JUNE 1 – SEPT. 20

Above: An old three-dimensional stereo viewing card depicts Old Faithful Geyser.

Left: A brochure published by the Northern Pacific Railroad promoted "The Land Of Geysers."

Facing page: Low clouds hang over the vast expanse of Hayden Valley.

Right: A Thomas Moran painting captured the Lower Falls of the Yellowstone River.

Below: A spring called the Punchbowl was photographed by William Jackson in 1902.

Park curio shops offered tourists many ready-made memories of Yellowstone.

Above: A burst of wildflowers revives a landscape blackened by the devastating fires of 1988.

Left: Elk graze against a backdrop of steaming thermal springs.

Tour boats took Park visitors for cruises on Yellowstone Lake.

A group of tourists winds its way along the boardwalk at Norris Geyser Basin.

A pond once graced the north entrance to Yellowstone Park at Gardiner, Montana.

62 Stoutest visitor of year, 308 lbs., 1922.-Linkey.

A scrapbook from 1922 showed that efforts at tourist data collection had reached an extreme.

A stereo viewing card shows a trainload of tourists arriving in Gardiner on their way to Yellowstone.

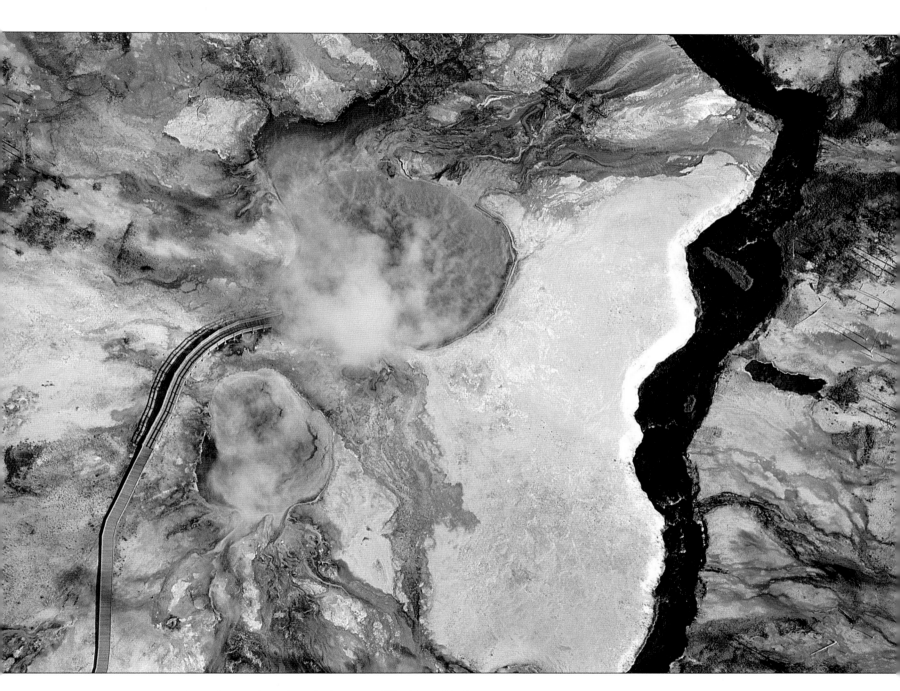

Steam billows from the colorful pools of Black Sand Basin.

Stagecoaches lined up for a photographic memory at Mammoth Hotel.

Come One, Come All

*A*ll in all, George Cowan's vacation to Yellowstone National Park had been going very well. Until the Indians shot him.

Part of a party of nine from the small Montana town of Radersburg, Cowan and his wife, Emma, had arrived at the national park (a ten-day trip by horse and wagon) five years after its creation. They were among the first true tourists to enjoy Yellowstone. There were no roads, no hotels and few trails—really, no improvements of any kind—but the Cowans and their cohorts had wild fun anyway. They caught, killed and devoured fresh fish and game, gobbled ripe berries and built big campfires at night. In an exercise that might now earn them a fine, they dumped all kinds of junk into the vent of Old Faithful. "We have filled it to the top with at least a thousand pounds of stones, trees, stumps, etc.," one of the nine wrote. The geyser spit it out. They then tried the same stunt with dirty clothes, which came out, they wrote in the parlance of the day, "nice and clean as a Chinaman could wash it with a week's scrubbing."

A band of tired, hungry and desperate Nez Perce Indians fleeing their reservations and the U.S. Army then ended up at the tourist party's camp in the Lower Geyser Basin.

There, Mr. Cowan excoriated the Indians and denied them food. In return, they shot him ("there was a flash, a deafening report, and a faint scream from my wife rang in my ears," he recalled later); the bullet flattened against his skull, doing little damage. Cowan came to only to get shot again, this time in the hip. When he next awoke, he crawled to his wrecked wagon and started a fire, but the fire flared up and burned his hands and knees. Soldiers finally found him, but in their eagerness to gawk at the geysers, left his wounds untended for hours. They later loaded him into a carriage, which flipped and rolled 300 feet down an embankment. When Cowan finally reached a hotel, an aide sat down on his bed to dress his wounds and—what else?—the bed broke and thumped to the floor.

A key to a room at Lake Hotel.

Emma Cowan afterwards blamed her husband's grumpiness for his wounds and won-

57

An embossed scrapbook held memories of "the wonders of geyserland" from 1918.

dered why the Indians were not more bloodthirsty "at a time when they must have hated the very name of the white race." At least Mr. Cowan had a sense of humor afterwards. He saved the bullet fired into his head and made it into a watch fob.

Visitors to Yellowstone National Park would rarely encounter as much adventure as the Cowans did—although a few fell prey to stagecoach holdups. But as their destination grew into a slice of true Americana, people would add a forceful new dimension to a realm long dominated by nature alone.

An early wood engraving by artist Thomas Moran shows a small party of people perched on a ledge above the yellow-red Grand Canyon of the Yellowstone. The view swallows their presence like the ocean would an ant on the beach. Only you know if it does the same for you.

Even today, those who tour Yellowstone have varying visions of what a national park should be. To some, it's a comfortable retreat from civilization. To others, a place offering scenery that is worth a roll of film. A place to see wildlife. To experience nature on nature's terms. To ponder an ever-changing geyser basin that transforms itself even as you wander through it. But to commoners like the Cowans who early on made their way to the newly flagged spot on the developing map of the West, Yellowstone was a profound prophecy without a clear purpose.

It took time for the public to grow accustomed to the notion of a national park, to see Yellowstone as its own. An 1883 camping trip through the park by President Chester Arthur, who caught 103 pounds of trout along the way, introduced the nation to the place. And if the citizenry did not know what the park should be, it at least had a good idea what the park should not be. A cartoon published in *Harper's Weekly* in 1883 warned of what "may be witnessed if the Yellowstone Park is leased to speculators." A crowd of top-hatted hawkers invite a startled visitor through a gate marked "Yellowstone Nat'l Park Co." Behind the hawkers is a sign: "Advertising to let, on the rocks, steam baths at the geysers." A placard says: "None but the company's carriages can enter this gate." Within the yellowed cartoon lurks an awareness that Yellowstone had a higher purpose. It was within the crucible of such

A stickpin souvenir.

scrutiny that the point—the aim—of the park began to take shape as slowly, carefully and deliberately as an arrowhead emerges, chip by chip, from a shapeless chunk of obsidian.

The point was there all along, but only time, talent and care could find it.

Rather than paying for more in a series of ineffective park superintendents who had been unwilling or unable to slow rampant wildlife poaching and vandalism, Congress finally refused to pay anything at all. And in 1886 the desperate Secretary of Interior turned to the nation's War Department for help. In came the U.S. Army, and assumed control.

Commanders very quickly concluded that perhaps the greatest pressure squeezing the park was its fans. Nobody in Yellowstone's history has found it easy to draw a sharp line between people's rightful enjoyment of the park and their infringement of the park's most basic values. But it was clear that if the park was to remain "a pleasuring ground for the benefit and enjoyment of the people," it must also be protected from them.

> *A very picturesque figure [wrote Captain George S. Anderson of the 6th Cavalry detachment assigned to Yellowstone] is a sentimental youth at twilight as he transmits his name to fame by writing on the "formations"—the hot springs deposits. A much more interesting figure is this same youth at sunrise the next morning, when, followed by a mounted soldier, he proceeds, scrub-brush and soap in hand, to the same spot and removes the perishable evidence of his late presence.*

The military brought discipline to the national park idea. Soldiers enforced regulations and caught Ed Howell, an infamous poacher who had been slaughtering bison in the Pelican Valley with repeating rifles. Since no laws specifically protected park wild-

A luggage tag souvenir.

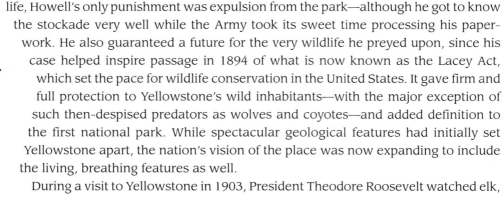

A Yellowstone Park souvenir letter opener.

life, Howell's only punishment was expulsion from the park—although he got to know the stockade very well while the Army took its sweet time processing his paperwork. He also guaranteed a future for the very wildlife he preyed upon, since his case helped inspire passage in 1894 of what is now known as the Lacey Act, which set the pace for wildlife conservation in the United States. It gave firm and full protection to Yellowstone's wild inhabitants—with the major exception of such then-despised predators as wolves and coyotes—and added definition to the first national park. While spectacular geological features had initially set Yellowstone apart, the nation's vision of the place was now expanding to include the living, breathing features as well.

During a visit to Yellowstone in 1903, President Theodore Roosevelt watched elk, pronghorn antelope, and deer. Bighorn sheep clambering up canyon walls provided him "a marvelous exhibition of climbing." He later wrote,

What has been actually accomplished in the Yellowstone Park affords the best possible object-lesson as to the desirability and practicability of establishing such wilderness reserves. This reserve is a natural breeding-ground and nursery for those stately and beautiful haunters of the wilds which have now vanished from so many of the great forests, the vast lonely plains, and the high mountain ranges, where they once abounded.

Fertilized by the nation's love for Yellowstone, and its willingness to spend money, rag-tag bunkhouses slapped together for the park's first visitors gave way to spectacular resort hotels that then grew amid Yellowstone's splendors. Hot spring water fed baths in the 143 rooms of the Fountain Hotel, built in 1890 overlooking the Lower Geyser Basin, but long since dismantled. At the same time, the colonial Lake Hotel rose on the northern shore of Yellowstone Lake.

Time and nature molded Yellowstone, but one architect molded its most palatial human additions. His name was Robert Reamer. He pieced together hotels that captivated their guests by reflecting their surroundings. Huge lobbies turned into spruced-up campfire circles where families mixed and reflected on the sights they had seen. It was a golden age of tourism. Reamer, barely more than 30, designed and supervised winter-long construction of the opulent Canyon Hotel, which opened in 1911 on the rim above the Yellowstone River but has since burned down. Its breakfast menu featured boiled salt mackerel, veal chops, fried calves liver and home-made sausage. Lodge employees performed skits in the evenings.

Perhaps the most treasured Reamer masterwork was and is the Old Faithful Inn, completed in 1904 at a cost of $200,000 and one of the few human-wrought edifices that could compare with the supernatural earthen creations that surround it. Its sharply peaked roof traces the outlines of distant mountaintops and the knotted, uneven logs and swirling burls of its wooden architecture reflect its tumultuous terrain, a terrain that never lets you forget where you are. Western novelist Owen Wister wrote:

I do not think that anybody there rejoiced quite as utterly as a boy employed in the hotel....We would be sitting tilted back, reading our mail, the tourists would have ceased talking and be lounging drowsily, the boy would be at the door, motionless as a set steel trap. Suddenly the trap would spring, the boy

The construction of elegant hotels, such as Old Faithful Inn, marked the dawning of a new era of tourism in Yellowstone Park.

would catapult into the door, and in his piping treble scream out:"Beehive's a-goin' off!" at which every tourist instantly started from his chair, and a leaping crowd gushed out of the hotel and sprinted down over the formation to catch the Beehive at it. Beehive finally quiescent, they returned slowly, sank into chairs and exhausted silence; you could have heard a mosquito. But the steel trap was again set, sprang soon, and again the silence was pierced: "There goes Old Faithful!"

It seems only human to try to spiff up nature—even when it is amply endowed all on its own. A handsome 1906 brochure produced by the Northern Pacific Railroad touted its route to the "Land of Geysers,"—"a land of pure, bracing and health-giving air, of sunlight and blue skies, a land which endows every visitor with an exhilarating physical inspiration which is closely akin to the elixir of life—the renewal of youth—which Ponce de Leon sought in vain more than a century ago."

What separated Yellowstone from other destinations of the time was that its elixir was not exclusive. It belonged to anyone and everyone. The Secretary of Interior had banned private enterprise "that will in any way prevent free access to...curiosities or springs." Tent campgrounds sprouted rows of candy-striped platform tents, low-income lodging options that panicked those catering to the upper crust. The president of the Northern Pacific Railroad worried that the proprietor of the camps "will in a short time run the first class business away from the park with the mobs he is taking in and the class of facilities people are putting up with." It was a sign that Yellowstone, once segregated by its remoteness, had moved within the reach of the common folk. And these working classes would give America's national parks their most powerful constituency. A visitor near the turn of the century wrote in her journal of the "genuine sons and daughters of the soil"—known in park lingo as "sagebrushers"—who first arrived in Yellowstone on "rustic" wagons drawn by worn farm animals.

A souvenir spoon shows the Lower Falls of the Yellowstone.

It was really strange to see how perfectly this class appreciates the wonders of the place and how glad they are to leave for a while their hard labor for the adventurous, the beautiful and the sublime. They always carried their outfit, camping every night. I have no doubt that they saw more and enjoyed more than conventional travelers.

More than anything else, the affordability and availability of the ultimate American workhorse—the automobile—would prove the comments true. Army commanders stationed in Yellowstone had for years resisted the internal combustion mechanisms, one of them arguing (backed by purveyors of private touring coaches) that their coughing and sputtering arrival would mark the first step in the commercialization of Yellowstone "that will make Coney Island look like a dime museum." When they could hold off cars no longer, soldiers enacted complex rules that limited motorized traffic to a maximum speed of 20 miles per hour and gave horses the right of way. In July 1915, the quintessential American transport—a Model T Ford—became the first automobile to pass through the park's gates.

A stagecoach carrying tourists in 1902 winds its way along a rugged road snaking between boulders.

William Jackson photographed the hot spring terraces above Mammoth in 1902.

Just Me In The Hammock.

An early tourist relaxes in a hammock at one of the Wylie tent camps.

It might not have been Coney Island, but suddenly Yellowstone had become a cherished part of America's backyard: a popular family playground where the kids, the deer and the antelope play.

Few people understood this better than a small but determined cadre eager to bring the multiplying number of national parks under unified management that could shepherd them through rapidly changing times. Led by well-to-do and energetic businessman Stephen T. Mather, they were more showmen then biologists, and perhaps rightly so, for they smoothly folded the national parks into the national heritage—giving the lands a solid foothold on the future. Mather pursued creation of an able National Park Service with boundless energy, spending his own money to whip up a publicity campaign. In August 1916, President Wilson signed a measure establishing the new agency, to administer the parks and, more specifically,

> to conserve the scenery and the natural and historic objects and the wild life therein and to provide for the enjoyment of the same in such manner and by such means as will leave them unimpaired for the enjoyment of future generations.

This then became the crux of the national parks. There may be no nobler order in the history of American conservation, and none as formidable. The instruction would ultimately pit visitors to Yellowstone against the sanctity of their beloved possession, forcing them to face up to the self-searching question of just who the parks are for.

"Our chief problem of the future will be in taking care of people," President Roosevelt had predicted during his visit, "because people are going to come whether we like it or not and it is up to us to look out for them."

People had to come, because the parks needed them. Only when they were commemorated by snapshots in photo albums and stickers on the bumpers of station wagons would the parks hold a secure spot in the nation's heart. So promoters trumpeted the scenery of the parks in a patriotic travel campaign they called "See America First." When Horace M. Albright, Mather's right-hand-man, hammered out guidelines for new park managers, he advised them to roll out the red carpet: "Every opportunity should be afforded the public, wher-

Souvenirs come in every shape and form.

64

OLD FAITHFUL GEYSER, YELLOWSTONE PARK--HAYNES PHOTO

My own dear
Lula. This is a picture of one of
the prettiest geyser's in the park
It is called Old Faithful. I sup-
pose by the time you get this

your birth day party will be.
over. I hope you all had a
good time and that you
liked your dolly dresses.
Be a good girly. Much love
& many kisses from Mama & Papa

Many a traveling "mama and papa" have dropped a line to children back home while they toured the Park.

Visitors stand silhouetted against the steam of Mammoth Hot Springs.

ever possible, to enjoy the national parks in the manner that best satisfies the individual taste. Automobiles and motorcycles will be permitted in all of the national parks; in fact, the parks will be kept accessible by any means practicable."

Rarely has a government initiative won over the country in such grand fashion. People embraced the parks and soon extended Yellowstone's protection to the jagged country that is now Grand Teton National Park. Yellowstone found itself an all-American vacation spot. The numbers entering its gates have had their ups and downs, particularly during the two world wars, but never have they mounted as dramatically as in the past few decades. From 10,769 at the turn of the century, they crested 1 million in 1948, hit 2 million in 1965 and 3 million in 1992.

We cannot give up our national parks, but in a way we must. It is not unusual today to hear park advocates talking of visitor limits: restraints on our affection. It may turn out to be the highest price we will have to pay to have Yellowstones.

They have become ever-precious islands of wildness that we have swamped with as much adoration as we have human-made wonders like the Sistine Chapel or the pyramids of Egypt. And yet in Yellowstone we do not celebrate our achievements—we celebrate something even greater, a place with a value that multiplies the rarer it becomes.

Old postcards show folks gathered like curious children around hot springs and geysers, in search of nature's Grail. They did what they wanted. There was Handkerchief Pool, a hot spring where "if you put a handkerchief in, the handkerchief would be sucked down and would come up in a few minutes nice and clean," a visitor wrote in 1888. (People tossed in more than handkerchiefs: a cleaning dredged up hair pins, nails, nuts and bolts and $1.98 in cash.) Skinny-dip in a pool. Bend a wire to spell out your name and place it in the outflow channels of the Mammoth Terraces, where mineral deposits would coat it in white, providing a distinctive souvenir in time for your departure.

Such is no longer possible.

With people came garbage. Smart on their feet, Yellowstone's black and grizzly bears found in the garbage a food source with modern, drive-thru convenience. And people found in the bears a source of entertainment. Tourists would gather in the cool evenings, sitting on bleachers in view of the dumps—in official lingo, "bear-feeding grounds." As one visitor staying at Canyon noted on a postcard, "about a mile from here, they put out food for the bears, and big and little ones come to eat. I counted 13 big bears and seven little ones one evening."

Without the benefit of history, it's difficult to see the future. So there was little way to know at the time that one of Yellowstone's top tourist spectacles would confound our modern conception of a national park.

Traffic jams proved the popularity of the dumps, steamrolling any reservations that the park had escaped the "natural condition" mandated for it. "Beggar bears" with nicknames like "Jesse James" sought handouts along park roads, where even President Harding tossed them snacks. Since coyotes, mountain lions and wolves killed photogenic elk, moose and

Canyon Hotel, with its elegant dining room overlooking the canyon, was abandoned in 1959 and destroyed by fire a year later.

bison, they in turn faced killing campaigns that ultimately exterminated the wolf from Yellowstone. Elk and bison enjoyed their own feeding grounds and ballooned in number. Anglers found better odds thanks to exotic fish species planted in park lakes and streams. Zoologists even tried to accentuate Yellowstone wildlife assemblage by releasing mountain goats and European antelope. They clearly did not belong, because they did not survive.

From our crow's nest on the mast of today, it's easy to assume such fiddling was somehow crude and ignorant because it altered nature's primeval layout. Wildlife science was indeed in its infancy then and there was somewhat less understanding that each of nature's components usually depends, in some way, on others. But the national parks themselves were still young and immature and were still seeking their purpose. It is easy now to oversimplify their purpose then.

Now, of course [wrote Albright, who succeeded the military as superintendent of Yellowstone], there would be a tremendous protest from the public if we did anything to interfere with the opportunity to see the bears. The Dudes and the Sagebrushers demand their bears. The present generation has been raised on bear stories, and real, live bears give them the thrill of their vacation. That is why they are the greatest single attraction in the national parks.

Albright had a pat, three-point answer for tourists who complained they had been scratched by bears while feeding them. First, he told them, they should not have gotten so close. Second, the wound was only superficial. Third, the bear bites were souvenirs better than any they could buy in a gift shop.

In popularizing itself, Yellowstone popularized its wildlife into American living rooms. There resided one Yogi Bear ("not just your average bear"), who romped through Jellystone Park, stealing "pick-ah-nick" baskets from gullible tourists.

A souvenir ash tray.

Sure, there were bears, and the bears performed on cue. There was Old Faithful, a spotlight trained on it during the night. Fires were extinguished before they turned the forest an unsightly black. Roads ran alongside the most popular, multicolored pools because that's what visitors wanted to see. Rangers kindly stampeded a herd of park buffalo for a key scene in the western movie *The Thundering Herd* because that's what the audience wanted.

What is more important, though, is that Yellowstone shined through whatever adornments we sought to hang on it. It was not necessarily the Yellowstone we see today, but one just as valuable, one that proved its worth to the people of the time, that surpassed our measures, that held up its promise of overpowering wildness. Even if management sanded down and polished the wild's sharp edges, Yellowstone projected its essence as powerfully as Old Faithful cleared its throat of the debris the Cowans and their friends had piled into it.

In the diary of his honeymoon to Yellowstone with his wife Estella, Alfred Bell described

U.S. Army Bicycle Corps crowded along Minerva Terrace, 1896.

his confrontation with the same canyon that had overpowered the human forms in Thomas Moran's early wood engraving:

> *Hastily alighting from our coaches we scramble with great caution down to the brink and look over, but we quickly draw back and grasp each other, the railing, or the rocks, or anything that has stability. That mighty rush of water seems like it would draw us with it. Speech is impossible. An immense volume of sound rises from the depths where that large river hurls itself to the rocks 140 feet below. As though satisfied with this last mighty effort the river now flows more gently on. But the road is far above it now, and every opening presents a picture more grandly beautiful than an artist's dream.*

A succession of mountain ridges rise behind Eagle Peak.

Onlookers gather to view the steaming spectacle of Old Faithful Geyser in this aerial view.

Fresh spring snow dampens a park road near Mammoth Hot Springs.

A herd of elk streams across the Lamar Valley with coyotes on alert for stragglers.

Left: Burned trees cast dark reflections across a Yellowstone pool.

Below: Wobbly bison calves signal spring in Yellowstone.

Early park visitors had no trouble catching as many trout as they wanted.

Park employees shovel snow from the roof of the first Canyon Hotel.

Horse and buggy traveler pauses before crossing Alum Creek Bridge about 1898.

WHERE GUSH THE
GEYSERS

OREGON SHORT LINE
ALL RAIL ROUTE TO THE
YELLOWSTONE

A flyer issued by the Oregon Short Line Railroad urges travelers to visit Yellowstone Park.

Left: Fireweed adds a spash of color to an area scorched by wildfire.

Below: Stands of trees stripe the undulating Pitchstone Plateau.

Scrapbook photos in the Park archives show tourists enjoying Yellowstone in its early days.

Tourists dance in the overflow from Great Fountain Geyser, circa 1910.

men Terrace

Tent of Ole Anderson,"Coated Specimens"
Showing Haynes studio adjoining house.
Old Cottage Hotel, built 1885

Early tourists stroll along Hymen Terrace near the Old Cottage Hotel, which was built in 1885.

Right: Hayden Survey members stand on the cone of Old Faithful Geyser in this first known photograph of the geological marvel.

Below: Tourists traveled in elegant six-horse-carriage style in olden days in Yellowstone.

Towering cliffs dwarf an old motor car bumping its way along primitive roads in the Park.

An elk with his antlers in velvet grazes amid the wildflowers of Yellowstone Park.

Changing Times

*I*t was afternoon and the sky was dark, but for a dawn-like glow above the pines. First came the noise, the sound of a thousand trains tearing down the tracks. Then came the flames, twisting tendrils of fire lashing the horizon. It was all the firefighters trying to protect the Old Faithful Inn could do to not drop their hoses and stand in awe of one of the wildest, most commanding visions the forest could conjure up: An unstoppable front of fire, exploding trees into orange pillars, fueling its own winds and weather, dropping cinders the size of baseballs and sweeping the length of a football field every minute.

While the marvelous Old Faithful Inn emerged unscathed, the epic forest fires that dominated Yellowstone during the summer of 1988 rattled America's conception of what its national parks should be. Sparked mainly by lightning and driven by dry, windy conditions, the blazes were largely natural, spectacular and even beneficial.

But they were not pretty.

It is this kind of contradiction that has forged a place for the national park idea in the modern age. If we want the parks to be natural, wild showcases, we must accept the natural unpredictability that comes with leaving them to themselves.

Fires in the summer of 1988 blackened more than 1 million acres in the Park.

Head of Yellowstone during the 1988 fires, Superintendent Bob Barbee faced a furnace of criticism for not protecting the national park from the forces of Nature, forces he still believes were unbeatable. He said,

> *The last thing that we learned is nature is not a gentle hostess. We had the best firefighting technology in the United States. And those professionals that manage wildfires were all here. And we got our tail kicked all over the map. There are circumstances beyond anybody's control.*

Our national parks, indeed, are playgrounds free of many of the constraints that bind the civilized world. But whether they are playgrounds for people or for Nature, or for some healthy combination of the two, is an open question that does not have a clear answer.

Today, people dominate much of Yellowstone's landscape. Walk through a campground in midsummer and you will see license plates from across the continent and beyond. Yellowstone's allure stretches that far. They come to see geysers, bears, moose, placid streams and forests, to be part of that milieu, rough edges and all. It is an allure that began when the tales first filtered out of the forested Yellowstone Plateau and has continued through all the twisting turns in its history. Human hands alone cannot create true wildness, but they can allow it to be.

In Yellowstone, they have.

Private enterprise tried many times to lasso Yellowstone's contents. Railroad boosters sought early on to ram a track through its boundaries. But affronts were rarely as bold as plans by agriculture interests and their allies in Congress to dam up park waterways. A dam finished in 1916 had enlarged Jackson Lake at the foot of the Grand Teton Mountains, prompting novelist Owen Wister to pause in his written recollections of Yellowstone "to lay

Travelers from around the world watch Old Faithful put on its famous show.

my ineffectual but heartfelt curse upon the commercial vandals who desecrated the outlet of Jackson's Lake with an ugly dam to irrigate some desert land away off in Idaho." Water was the key to settlement of the arid West and those who needed it to fill their furrows next turned to Yellowstone: as they saw it, dams harnessing Yellowstone's wild streams would better the park by making it more productive. Ambitious plans outlined a dam that would restrain the myriad waterfalls in the park's little-known southwest tip, called the Cascade Corner, and another that would undermine the Continental Divide by enlarging Yellowstone Lake and diverting much of the excess water through a subterranean tunnel under the Divide (excavated rock would be used to pave park roads) and into southern Idaho.

Plans to crosscut Yellowstone with concrete tested the resolve of the new and tenuous National Park Service. In a loss that had left environmentalists reeling, a dam authorized in 1913 had flooded Yosemite National Park's pristine Hetch Hetchy Valley a few years before the agency's creation. New Director Stephen T. Mather and Yellowstone chief Horace M. Albright would not let it happen again. An encoded telegram alerted Albright that the federal Reclamation Service would need pack horses and boats to survey Yellowstone for the grand dams. He promptly sent all horses out of the park and ordered all boats into storage. Instructed to draw up a favorable report on the proposal, Albright shoved the file into the trash and blamed its disappearance on the janitor. Putting his job on the line for the sake of Yellowstone, Mather wrote to the Secretary of Interior:

Shoshone Lake darkens as the sun fades beyond the western horizon.

An old Union Pacific Railway placard advertises the wildlife and scenery of Yellowstone.

Is there not some place in this great nation of ours where lakes can be preserved in their natural state; where we and all generations to follow us can enjoy the beauty and charm of mountain waters in the midst of primeval forests? The country is large enough to spare a few such lakes and beauty spots. The nation has wisely set apart a few national parks where a state of nature is to be preserved. If the lakes and forests of these parks cannot be spared from the hand of commercialization, what hope can there be for the preservation of any scenic features of the mountains in the interest of posterity?

One after another, the dam plans broke down, and their fragments cemented the foundation of the national parks. The United States, wrote Interior Secretary Ray Lyman Wilbur in 1931, "should be the last one to attempt to mar or destroy any portion of this magnificent wilderness area, perhaps the most important natural heritage we can preserve for posterity in this country."

Yellowstone is our natural heritage, if we know what natural means. Because there is a fine but distinctive difference between a wild Yellowstone and a managed Yellowstone.

It's the difference between a carefully mowed and manicured lawn and an unkempt alpine meadow that explodes into color for a few summer months. The lawn is pleasing to the eye, its grass evenly clipped, its fountain dripping a staccato rhythm. But the meadow transcends that measured, linear and symmetrical threshold to achieve the real definition of beauty. Its splendor does not lie in any one element: a butterfly perched on a wildflower, pine needles piled on the ground, lichen coloring a piece of granite. It lies instead in the mingling of all the elements in all their shifting, uneasy variety: water splashing over smooth stones, a woodpecker clacking against a tree trunk, aspen leaves fluttering and a rock tumbling under the toes of a marmot. It lies in the simple realization that you never know what will happen next.

A stereo viewing card shows the Grand Canyon of the Yellowstone.

Yellowstone is like that.

It is not so much the raw elements—the grizzly bears, geysers and spectacular country—that make it a national park. It is how we value the elements and the natural scene they comprise. What sets it apart from the static displays of a natural history museum is its fascinating insistence on change—constant change that, like an ever-turning kaleidoscope, never enacts the same pattern twice.

It challenges our senses in a way that the predictability that once defined Yellowstone could not.

There were the bears, addicted to the garbage dumps. Buried in the cabinets of Yellowstone's archives is a collection of postcards. One of them, its single, one-cent stamp

Tourists and bears developed nasty habits in the Park's earlier days.

postmarked in 1934, reads: "A bear upset our victuals yesterday—they are too friendly here."

Too friendly. In its uncertain youth, Yellowstone at some points, in some ways, began to resemble a zoo. Which, perhaps, was not all bad. Poachers had exacted such a toll on the park's wildlife in early years that the only way to save a sample of the native species was to provide irrigated fields where they could feed under guard. After the profit-driven slaughter of the millions of buffalo that had roamed the western plains and all but about 50 park bison, Army officers established a captive herd and used its offspring to repopulate Yellowstone with what is now one of the largest free-roaming buffalo herds anywhere. After park keepers exterminated wolves and reduced the numbers of other predators, the elk population boomed and during tough winters, thousands of elk died. To avoid such unpleasant spectacles, Congress and wildlife groups did what they thought was right: they pitched in to buy supplemental feed.

While the scenery looked grand and the number of visitors continued its steep climb to today, though, the fundamental ecological gears that drive Yellowstone started jamming.

Biologists determined the rapidly multiplying elk were mowing down park rangelands, so rangers shot and captured nearly 20,000 of the animals between 1934 and 1962. The elk responded by reproducing even faster. So rangers shot more. The slaughter stopped only when studies began to imply that the range was failing not so much because of hungry elk, but because fires that would have naturally opened up new grazing lands had been unnaturally suppressed under the stern doctrine of Smokey Bear.

It was a hint of the latest and perhaps most dramatic refinement of the national park ideal. Rarely does Nature operate on clear causes and effects. What looks like a simple elk versus grass relationship may be fire versus forests versus grass versus elk versus vegetarian rodents versus birds of prey versus fish versus streams versus weather—and even that does not do justice to the intricacies of natural systems we are still trying to interpret. It is a testament to our willingness to learn from these systems that we have gradually recognized that to operate most effectively, they need to govern their own future. And within the last few decades, national parks have become places where they are left to themselves, where we stand in awe of such systems without sticking our fingers into the works.

Debate that still rages over the question of whether elk continue overgrazing Yellowstone honors the park as one of the few places where we can watch, study and debate the way the world really works.

As one who had himself killed wolves, the famed, late naturalist Aldo Leopold realized too late the "modern curse of excess deer and elk" that appeared in the absence of predators that would normally cull them. If there were any place in the United States that predators like wolves could still roam and hunt as they had for ages, he proclaimed, it ought to be Yellowstone.

So echoed his son, A. Starker Leopold, who led a panel of independent biologists who in 1963 formalized the hands-off, let-nature-take-its-course philosophy that

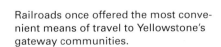

Railroads once offered the most convenient means of travel to Yellowstone's gateway communities.

Fires blossomed in the night along the Gibbon River in the summer of 1988, one of the worst fire seasons in the Park's history.

governs national parks to this day. "If the goal cannot be fully achieved it can be approached," they advised the Secretary of Interior. "A reasonable illusion of primitive America could be recreated."

Like an aged ship rattling and shuddering, the National Park Service shifted course. No longer did rangers feed or cull elk. Garbage dumps were closed and fenced to keep bears out; rules against feeding bears were actively enforced. Main roads were routed away from fragile hot springs. When disease afflicted wildlife, it was allowed to run its course. Fires sparked by lightning could burn so long as they did not threaten structures. Predators got a new lease on life—and in 1995, the government spent millions to undo its longstanding anti-predator policy by releasing wolves that are now recolonizing Yellowstone.

It was not always easy.

It's not easy to stand on the sidelines as a spectator, and see elk starve to death. Outrage flew like a winter storm when park rangers would not rescue a bison from a frozen pond where it would, and did, die. It was not easy in 1988 for those who love Yellowstone to watch flames leap and skip through lodgepole forests, etching abstract patterns of black for anyone watching from above. They had no choice. That was the year Nature took the free hand we gave her and ran with it, shoving us aside, defying modern technology, fleets of airplanes, crack firefighting squads and even the U.S. Army and Marine Corps—as she enforced our own mandate to leave her alone.

It was not easy for those who earn their livings by serving Yellowstone visitors to see tourist cabins at Fishing Bridge demolished as the popular visitor complex at Fishing Bridge was ceded back to the grizzlies. The government's decision to return wolves to Yellowstone came only after rancorous de-

Forest fires race along the ridgelines south of West Yellowstone, Montana, in 1988.

bate that shook the nation from one end to the other. And it was by no means easy for ranchers living on private land around Yellowstone to watch resignedly as federal agencies in 1995 repopulated the national park with its top predator, a predator they knew would, at least on occasion, leave the park and kill their livestock.

But they are all decisions America has made.

What has become most apparent as the cogs and wheels that drive Yellowstone grind forward was that as idealistic as it might seem, we cannot leave Yellowstone to itself. It needs us. It needs our respect. It's not possible to run a blade along Yellowstone's border on a map, lift the park out and ignore the rest. Gears inside the park connect to gears outside the park, which ultimately connect to us.

Ecosystem is the modern buzzword for such interaction; an ecosystem is defined by

Winter snows stretch toward the summit of Turret Mountain near the southeast boundary of Yellowstone Park.

nature's components, not by a line on a map. Most simply, it's defined by a young grizzly bear, born in a musty underground den in Yellowstone, exiting the park and foraging for forbs in a meadow within one of the national forests that surround it. We play a more active role in managing the forests, where logging, livestock grazing and mining are allowed, but they remain part of the whole. While the park is a final stronghold of grizzlies, bison and others—the core of the largest intact ecosystem in the temperate zones of the Earth—the bear needs more than the park to survive. That young, cinnamon-furred cub cannot wander on forever in search of greener pasture, but it can try. And in this way, no matter how distant we are, Yellowstone will always be reaching out to us.

Which brings us back to the question of who Yellowstone is for. In the long view, we did not create Yellowstone for ourselves, or for the wildlife. We created it for the future.

A souvenir plate.

One force determines whether Yellowstone can stay true to the "natural condition" mandated by the act that created it 125 years ago—and whether it can reflect "primitive America."

Us.

We are coming to Yellowstone in numbers we never have before, numbers that would have swamped Mather and Albright and their "See America First" slogan. Roads first set down in the park's Army days are disintegrating under today's traffic like snow in the summer sun. Exhaust from snowmobiles exceeds pollution standards on some winter days, forcing park keepers to contemplate limits on snowmobile numbers. Tapping geysers in other regions has dried them up; there is talk of similar tinkering near Yellowstone. Grizzly bears may seem all-powerful, but they need peace and quiet, too—so signs now declare bear haunts off-limits to people at certain times of the year. But it's also possible to find solace in our numbers. About a quarter of all Americans have toured Yellowstone. Moreover, a national poll a few years ago found that nearly 90 percent of all Americans want to visit Yellowstone, although many know they probably never will.

There may be no greater measure of the park's worth than this: The simple pleasure of knowing Yellowstone exists means something, even to those who may never experience it.

They want to know that Old Faithful's watery blasts will remain one of the most recognizable sights on the continent. They want to know there is still a place where we can learn from the world.

Hiding in the steaming pools framing geysers and springs are microscopic organisms that were unknown when Yellowstone was set aside. Today they are at the forefront of technology. A microbe from Yellowstone holds the ingredient that makes DNA fingerprinting possible, that produces the most accurate disease diagnoses known today, that forms the foundation of the world's biotechnology industry.

Another hot-water microbe is more closely related to the first life on Earth than anything else known today. Looking into the blue-green pools is like looking into the planet's past.

They exist because Yellowstone exists.

If we wonder about practices in Yellowstone's past, people 125 years from now might wonder about our practices. Perhaps they will frown on automobiles rolling through the park and will instead experience a virtual Yellowstone constructed by technology.

One hopes not. Nothing can equal the tingling spray of a geyser wafting across your face, of hooking a wild cutthroat trout, of spying wolves as they make a kill, of halting your travels in deference to a half-ton bison.

Water fired from Old Faithful's subterranean plumbing today fell as rain more than 500 years ago. The drops that fall today will seep into the earth, filter into Old Faithful's conduit to the surface and erupt hundreds of years from now as a new generation of park lovers reveres a place where they do not reign.

John Muir, a man of the mountains who watched his beloved Hetch Hetchy Valley drown, found hope in Yellowstone. Update a few of his figures and his words still hold true today:

> Even in these cold, doubting, questioning, scientific times many of the Yellowstone fountains seem able to work miracles. Near the Prismatic Spring is the great Excelsior Geyser, which is said to throw a column of boiling water 60 to 70 feet in diameter to a height of from 50 to 300 feet, at irregular periods. This is the greatest of all the geysers yet discovered anywhere. The Firehole River, which sweeps past it, is, at ordinary stages, a stream about 100 yards wide and 3 feet deep; but when the geyser is in eruption, so great is the quantity of water discharged that the volume of the river is doubled, and it is rendered too hot and rapid to be forded.
>
> ...Few tourists, however, will see the Excelsior in action, or a thousand other interesting features of the park that lie beyond the wagon-roads and the hotels. The regular trips—from three to five days—are too short. Nothing can be done at a speed of forty miles a day. The multitude of mixed, novel impressions rapidly piled on one another make only a dreamy, bewildering, swirling blur, most of which is unrememberable. Far more time should be taken. Walk away quietly in any direction and taste the freedom of the mountaineer. Camp out among the grass and gentians of glacier meadows, in craggy garden nooks full of Nature's darlings. Climb the mountains and get their good tidings. Nature's peace will flow into you as sunshine flows into trees. The winds will blow their own freshness into you, and the storms their energy, while cares will drop off like autumn leaves, As age comes on, one source of enjoyment after another is closed, but Nature's sources never fail. Like a generous host, she offers here brimming cups in endless variety, served in a grand hall, the sky its ceiling, the mountains its walls, decorated with glorious paintings and enlivened with bands of music ever playing. The petty discomforts that beset the awkward guest, the unskilled camper, are quickly forgotten, while all that is precious remains. Fears vanish as soon as one is fairly free in the wilderness.

The turquoise blossom of Morning Glory Pool has enthralled Park visitors for more than a century.

Mineral deposits laced the edges of Sapphire Pool in this photograph taken by William Jackson in the late 1800s.

Above: The coyote is one of the many forms of wildlife that abound in Yellowstone Park.

Left: The Madison River is one of the world's blue-ribbon trout streams.

YELLOWSTONE PARK

GRAND CANYON OF THE YELLOWSTONE

NORTHERN PACIFIC RAILWAY

A railroad brochure from 1915 shows the Lower Falls of the Yellowstone.

1008. LIBERTY CAP—EXTINCT GEYSER CONE.

A stereo viewing card shows the Liberty Cap, the mineral formation constructed by a former hot spring.

A crater of bubbling mud hisses and spits in this 1902 photo by William Jackson.

Right: A marmot peeks over the edge of a boardwalk, watching tourists for any hint of a meal.

Below: Billowing steam shrouds visitors to Midway Geyser Basin.

100

Sinuous fingers of the Madison River curve through meadows near West Yellowstone, Montana.

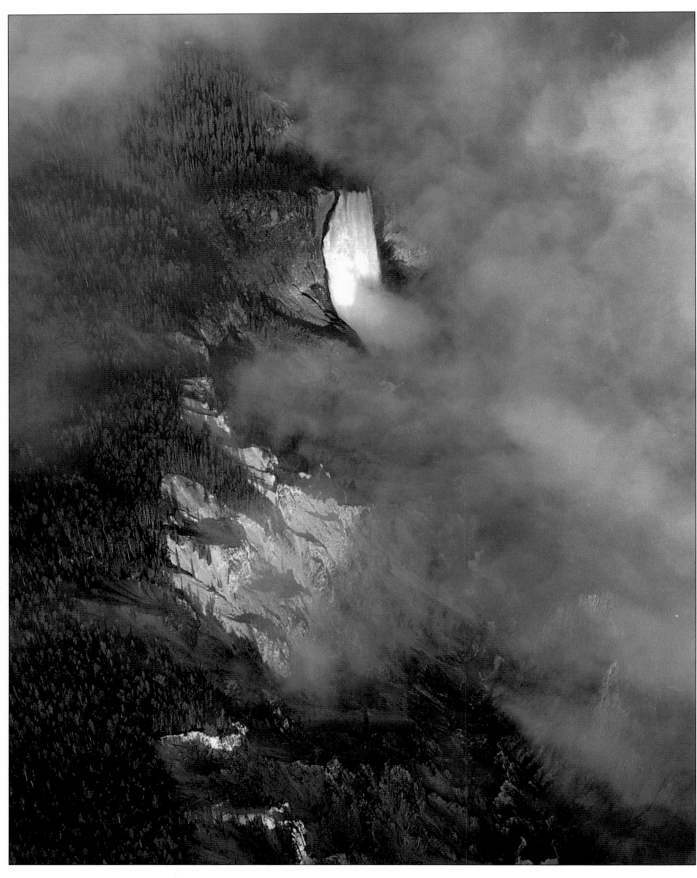

Mist covers the Grand Canyon of the Yellowstone below the Lower Falls.

Fresh snow outlines trees on Dunraven Pass.

Mrs. A. K. Noyes

Adilade Bestick

on top of Old Faithful Inn

Mrs. A. K. Noyes

"The Inn" Entrance

Above: Stevenson Island slices the surface of Yellowstone Lake at sunrise.

Facing page: A personal scrapbook holds images of an early visit to Old Faithful Inn.

Above: A bighorn sheep, its curling horns highlighted by the sun, stands atop a ridge in Yellowstone.

Right: Colter Peak rises to 10,683 feet in the Park's roadless southeastern wilderness.

The Pulpit Terraces form steps to the sky at Mammoth Hot Springs in this 1902 photograph by William Jackson.

"Where Gush The Geysers" proclaims an old travel brochure from the Oregon Short Line Railroad.

146   The Old Trestle, Golden Gate Canyon.

A stereo viewing card hints at the precariousness of a horse-drawn trip through the Golden Gate.

Human figures are dwarfed by nature's gigantic terraces at Mammoth Hot Springs.

Acknowledgements

We would like to thank the Public Affairs Offices of both the National Park Service and Yellowstone National Park, especially Marsha Karle and Cheryl Matthews, for their invaluable assistance in the preparation of this book.

We would like to offer a special thank you to Mike Finley, superintendent of Yellowstone National Park, and his staff, without whose help this book commemorating the 125th anniversary of Yellowstone Park could not have been possible.

Credits

Photographs on the following pages depict items in the historical archives of the United States Department of the Interior, National Park Service, Yellowstone National Park: front and back covers, 1, 2, 3, 5, 8, 11, 13, 14, 16, 18, 20, 22, 23, 24 (2), 25, 26 (2), 30, 31, 33, 34 (2), 36 (2), 37, 39, 40, 43, 44, 47 (2), 48 (2), 49, 53 (2), 54 (2), 57, 58, 59 (2), 60, 62, 63 (2), 64 (2), 65, 67, 68, 74, 76, 78, 79, 80 (2), 86, 87, 89, 93, 95 (2), 98, 99 (2), 104, 108, 109 (2), 110, 111, 112.

Photographs on the following pages were provided through the courtesy of the Montana Historical Society and came from the Society's Haynes Photographic Collection: 10, 15, 35, 52, 56, 61, 69, 74, 81, 88, 89.

Photographs on the following pages were taken by *Billings Gazette* Chief Photographer Larry Mayer: 6-7, 9, 17, 21, 27, 28-29, 32, 38, 40-41, 42, 46-47, 50-51, 55, 66, 70, 71 (2), 72, 73 (2), 77 (bottom), 84, 85, 90, 91, 92, 96-97, 100 (bottom), 101, 102, 104-105, 106, 107.

Photographs on the following pages were taken by *Billings Gazette* Photographer Bob Zellar: 4, 7, 12, 19, 45, 51, 77 (top), 82, 83, 100 (top), 103.

The quotation from Owen Wister's "Old Yellowstone Days" on pages 60 and 62 is reprinted with permission of the publisher: Copyright © 1936 by *Harper's Magazine*. All rights reserved.

Members of the 1871 Hayden Survey team prepare to continue their exploration of Yellowstone.

For Further Reading

The Bears of Yellowstone. Paul Schullery. Yellowstone Library and Museum Association. Yellowstone National Park, Wyo. 1980.

The Birth of the National Park Service: The Founding Years, 1913-1933. Horace M. Albright as told to Robert Cahn. Howe Brothers, Salt Lake City, 1985.

Camping Out in The Yellowstone, 1882. Mary Bradshaw Richards. University of Utah Press, Salt Lake City, Utah.

The Discovery of Yellowstone Park: Journal of the Washburn Expedition to the Yellowstone and Firehole Rivers in the Year 1870. Nathaniel Pitt Langford. University of Nebraska Press, Lincoln, Nebraska, 1972.

Ferdinand Vandiveer Hayden and the Founding of Yellowstone National Park. U.S. Department of the Interior, Geological Survey. U.S. Government Printing Office, Washington, D.C., 1980.

The Geysers of Yellowstone, 3rd ed. T. Scott Bryan. University Press of Colorado, Niwot, Colorado, 1995.

Mirror of America: Literary Encounters with the National Parks. David Harmon, ed. Roberts Rinehart Publishers, Boulder, Colorado, 1989.

My Yellowstone Years. Donald C. Stewart. Wilderness Adventure Books, Fowlerville, Michigan, 1989.

Oh, Ranger! A Book About the National Parks. Horace M. Albright and Frank J. Taylor. Outbooks, Golden, Colorado, 1980.

Old Yellowstone Days. Edited by Paul Schullery. Colorado Associated University Press, Boulder, Colorado, 1979.

Old Yellowstone Views. John F. Barber. Mountain Press Publishing Co., Missoula, Montana, 1987.

Saving All the Parts. Rocky Barker. Island Press, Washington, D.C., 1993.

The Place Where Hell Bubbled Up: A History of the First National Park. David A. Clary. Homestead Publishing, Moose, Wyoming, 1993.

The Plainsmen of the Yellowstone: A History of the Yellowstone Basin. Mark H. Brown. University of Nebraska Press, Lincoln, Nebraska, 1961.

Promise or Threat? A Study of "Greater Yellowstone Ecosystem" Management. George Reynolds. Westerners Concerned About Resources and Environment, Riverton, Wyoming, 1987.

A Trip to The Yellowstone National Park in July, August, and September, 1875. General W.E. Strong, With an Introduction by Richard A. Bartlett. University of Oklahoma Press, Norman, Oklahoma, 1968.

The Valley of the Upper Yellowstone: An Exploration of the Headwaters of the Yellowstone River in the Year 1869. As recorded by Charles W. Cook, David E. Folsom, and William Peterson. University of Oklahoma Press, Norman, Oklahoma, 1965.

Yellowstone: A Wilderness Besieged. Richard A. Bartlett. University of Arizona Press, Tucson, Arizona, 1985.

Yellowstone: Land of Fire and Ice. Gretel Ehrlich. HarperCollins Publishers, New York, New York, 1995.

Yellowstone National Park: Historical and Descriptive. Marie M. Augspurger. The Naegele-Auer Printing Co., Middletown, Ohio, 1948.

Yellowstone On Fire! Robert Ekey and the Staff of the Billings Gazette. The Billings Gazette, Billings, Montana, 1989.

Yellowstone Pioneers: The Story of the Hamilton Stores and Yellowstone National Park. Gwen Petersen. Produced for Hamilton Stores Inc. by Sequoia Communications, Santa Barbara, California, 1985.

Yellowstone Place Names. Lee H. Whittlesey. Montana Historical Society Press, Helena, Montana, 1988.

The Yellowstone Story: A History of Our First National Park, Volumes One and Two. Aubrey L. Haines. Yellowstone Library and Museum Association in Cooperation with Colorado Associated University Press, Yellowstone National Park, Wyoming, 1977.

Michael Milstein, author of *Yellowstone: 125 Years of America's Best Idea,* has been covering Wyoming and Yellowstone National Park for *The Billings Gazette* since 1989. He is also the author of *Wolf: Return To Yellowstone,* which was published in 1995 by *The Billings Gazette.* His reporting has won awards from the Montana Newspaper Association and from the Society of Professional Journalists. He won the Ray Bruner Science Writing Award in 1994 for articles on microbes of Yellowstone hot springs. He has been named environmental writer of the year by both the Greater Yellowstone Coalition and the Wyoming Wildlife Federation. A 1988 graduate of Duke University, Milstein has reported for the *Los Angeles Times,* the *Sacramento Bee,* and the Raleigh, North Carolina, *News and Observer.* He has also written for *Reader's Digest, Outside, Science, National Parks,* the *San Diego Union-Tribune,* the *Boston Globe,* the *Christian Science Monitor* and *High Country News.* Milstein and his wife, Sue, live in Cody, Wyoming.